Stepping Out Of The Rabbit Hole

Daniel J Warner

CONTENTS

1 THE DESCENT

It was a wild ride, my dive into the rabbit hole. I was on a journey, an odyssey through the vast, electric sea of the internet. And once you dive in, it's not always easy to find your way back out. The allure of the endless information, the constant buzz of connectivity, luring you deeper and deeper into the depths. It's a seductive call, promising knowledge, and belonging, but it's a call that can lead you astray, pulling you away from the solid ground of reality and into a world of illusions.

It all started with a click, just a tiny little click. It was the catalyst that stirred some deep passion within me. Before I knew it, I was hooked, tumbling down the rabbit hole of information and connectivity. At first, it was exhilarating - the people, the ideas, the never-ending buzz of it all. It was as if I had tapped into a great secret, a hidden truth that the mainstream just couldn't grasp. I felt like a pioneer, a digital explorer charting new territories and uncovering the mysteries of the online world. The rush of discovery, the thrill of being part of something bigger than myself, it was intoxicating.

I remember those early days, those first forays into the digital frontier. It was a time of wonder, of possibility. Every new link, every new social media post, it was like a doorway into a hidden world, a secret group of like-minded souls. I would spend hours, days, lost in the labyrinth of information, chasing down every lead, every whisper of truth.

And the connections I made, the people I met, it was like finding a long-lost tribe. These were people who understood me, who shared my thirst for knowledge, my suspicion of the mainstream narrative. We would talk for hours, sharing our discoveries, our theories, our visions of a world beyond the veil of illusion.

But even then, even in those early days of innocence and excitement, there were warning signs, little red flags that I chose to ignore. The endless suspicion, the absolutism of the thinking. It was like they were operating on a different plane of reality, one where everything was a conspiracy, where nothing was as it seemed.

I brushed it off at first, chalking it up to the passion of the newly awakened. After all, hadn't I felt that same rush of righteous indignation, that same sense of being one of the select few who knew the truth? But as time went on, as I sank deeper into the digital abyss, those red flags became harder and harder to ignore.

But the internet, it's a wild trip. There's a tipping point, a moment where the tide turns, and suddenly you're not just exploring anymore - you're drowning. And that's exactly what happened to me. The more I delved, the more I discovered, the more I realized just how deep this rabbit hole could be. It was a labyrinth of information, a maze of conspiracies and alternate realities that seemed to stretch on forever. Each new piece of information, each new theory, was like a breadcrumb trail, leading me further and further away from the path of reason.

I didn't realize it at the time, but I was being sucked into a vortex of disinformation, a whirlpool of suspicion and distrust. The more time I spent online, the more I felt my grip on reality slipping. The real world, with all its nuance and complexity, began to feel distant, unreal. The only thing that felt solid, that felt true, was the world I had constructed for myself in the echo chambers of the internet.

It was the algorithms, those guiding forces, that led me astray. They started feeding me a steady diet of fear and distrust, until I was seeing conspiracies in every shadow. And the more I clicked, the more I watched, the deeper I sank into this echo chamber of madness. It was like being caught in a whirlpool, each click pulling me further from the shore of reason and into the swirling depths of suspicion. The algorithms, they're designed to keep us engaged, to keep us clicking, to keep us consuming. But in doing so, they can also lead us down wayward paths, into echo chambers where our beliefs are reinforced and our doubts are silenced.

I didn't want to see it at first, didn't want to admit that I had become a prisoner of my own confirmation bias. But the evidence was mounting, becoming harder and harder to ignore. The way I would seek out information that confirmed my beliefs, while dismissing anything that challenged them. The way I would feel a rush of righteousness, of validation, every time I found a new piece of "proof" to support my theories.

And the communities I was a part of, the online spaces I inhabited, they only served to reinforce this echo chamber mentality. These were spaces where dissent was not tolerated, where anyone who questioned the prevailing narrative was shouted down, ridiculed, cast out. It was a world of us versus them, of the enlightened few against the brainwashed masses.

Soon, I was cutting ties with anyone who tried to throw me a lifeline. Friends, family, anyone who dared to question my newfound "truth". I was alone, prowling the digital wilderness, convinced that I was one of the few who really understood what was going on. It was a lonely existence, but in my mind, it was a necessary one. I believed that I was part of a select few, a group of enlightened individuals who had seen beyond the veil of mainstream lies and deception.

But the price of this "enlightenment" was steep. I found myself growing more and more isolated, more and more disconnected from the real world. My relationships suffered, my work suffered, my mental health suffered. I was consumed by the need to be right, to prove to everyone that I knew the truth.

And yet, even as I sank deeper into this morass of conspiracy and delusion, there was a part of me that knew something was wrong. A small voice of reason, a flicker of doubt that I couldn't quite extinguish. It was like a splinter in my mind, an unshakeable sense that I had wandered too far from the path of sanity.

In the depths of that abyss, that nagging voice in the back of my head, a tiny spark, fighting to be heard above the noise. And it was asking me the most important question of all:

How did I end up here?

How did I go from a curious explorer to a distrustful recluse, cut off from the real world and lost in a sea of digital delusions? It was a question I had been avoiding, a question I didn't want to face. Because deep down, I knew the answer. I had allowed myself to be led astray, to be seduced by conspiracy and mistrust.

That question, it was like a lifeline, a tether to reality that I clung to in my darkest moments. It was the thread that would eventually lead me out of the labyrinth, back to the light of reason and truth. But the journey back, it was not an easy one. It was a struggle, a battle against the very habits of mind that had led me astray in the first place.

That question, it was a beacon in the darkness. A guiding light, leading me back to the surface. And the journey back - it was a struggle, a battle against the currents of disinformation and manipulation. It was like swimming upstream, fighting against the flow of lies and half-truths that threatened to pull me back under. Every step was a challenge, every moment a test of my resolve. But I knew I had to keep going, I had to find my way back to the world of the real.

I had to relearn how to think critically, how to question my own assumptions and biases. I had to seek out information from a variety of sources, not just those that confirmed my preexisting beliefs. I had to learn to be comfortable with uncertainty, with the idea that the truth is not always simple or straightforward.

And I had to reconnect with the people in my life, the ones who had been trying to reach me all along. I had to learn to listen, really listen, to perspectives that differed from my own. I had to rebuild the bridges I had burned in my pursuit of digital "truth".

But I made it. I stepped out of the rabbit hole, back onto the solid ground of reality. And now, I'm here to share the tale, to light the way for any other lost souls out there who might be drowning in the digital deep. Because if there's one thing I learned on this crazy trip, it's that the truth - the real truth - it's not always easy to find. But it's always worth seeking. It's worth fighting for, worth struggling for, worth risking everything for. Because without truth, without a firm grasp on reality, we're just leaves in the wind, blown about by every passing breeze of misinformation and manipulation.

It's not an easy journey, this path back to sanity. It requires constant vigilance, constant questioning of our own beliefs and assumptions. It requires the humility to admit when we're wrong, the courage to face uncomfortable truths. But it's a journey we must all undertake if we hope to navigate this new digital landscape with our minds intact.

We're about to embark on a wild ride through the twists and turns of the information age. And when we come out the other side, we just might find ourselves standing on solid ground once again. The road ahead is winding and uncertain, but the destination - a clear mind and a firm grasp on reality - is worth every bump and detour along the way. It won't be easy, and there will be times when the siren's song of the internet will try to lure us back into the depths. But if we hold fast to the truth, to the things we know to be real and true, we can navigate this digital landscape without losing ourselves in the process.

Because in the end, that's what this journey is all about - finding ourselves, our true selves, amidst the noise and the chaos of the online world. It's about learning to separate the signal from the static, the truth from the lies, and emerging from the rabbit hole with our sanity intact. It's about reconnecting with the world around us, with the people and the experiences that make life worth living. It's about rediscovering the joy and the beauty that exists beyond the screen, in the tangible, tactile world of the real.

The digital world, for all its wonders and possibilities, can also be a hall of mirrors, a labyrinth of illusions that distorts our perception of reality. It's up to us to learn to navigate this maze, to find our way back to the true north of reason and facts. It's up to us to create online spaces that foster genuine connection and understanding, rather than division and mistrust.

And it's up to us to remember, always, the primacy of the real world, the world of face-to-face interactions and lived experiences. The digital realm, for all its allure, is ultimately a tool, a means to an end. It's not a substitute for the richness and complexity of real life.

So let's take that first step, together, and see where this wild ride takes us. The descent may have been harrowing, but the ascent - the return to the light - that's where the real adventure begins. It's a journey of self-discovery, of growth, of transformation. And it's a journey that we all must take, in our own way and in our own time. But know this: no matter how deep you've fallen, no matter how lost you may feel, there is always a way back. There is always hope, always a chance for redemption and renewal.

The rabbit hole, it's a seductive place. It promises hidden knowledge, secret truths, a sense of belonging. But in the end, it's a trap, a dead end that leads only to isolation and delusion. The real truth, the real knowledge, the real connections - those are found in the light of day, in the messy, complicated, beautiful world of reality.

So let us emerge from the depths, let us shake off the shadows of the rabbit hole. Let us rediscover the joy of authentic human connection, the thrill of genuine discovery, the deep satisfaction of a mind in harmony with reality.

The descent is over; the ascent awaits. Let us rise, together, and greet the dawn of a new day. A day of clarity, of truth, of renewed hope and possibility. The journey ahead may be challenging, but it's a journey worth taking. For at the end of it lies not just a clearer understanding of the world, but a clearer understanding of ourselves.

And so, I invite you to join me on this journey, to step out of the rabbit hole and into the light. It won't be easy, but it will be worth it. For in the end, we'll emerge stronger, wiser, and more alive than ever before.

We'll have faced the darkness and come out the other side, ready to embrace the beauty and the wonder of the world anew. So let us begin, let us take that first step, and let us see where this wild, wonderful journey takes us. A new day awaits, and with it, the promise of a brighter, more authentic future. Let us seize it, together, with open hearts and minds. The ascent begins now.

2 THE ECHO CHAMBER

The rabbit hole, it pulls you in with whispers of hidden knowledge and secret truths. It's a trip, a wild ride into a world where everything you thought you knew gets flipped on its head. And once you're in, once you've taken that first hit of alternative facts and conspiracy theories, it's hard to find your way back out.

I fell deep into that abyss, lost myself in the labyrinth of online echo chambers and digital landscapes. It was a rush at first, feeling like I was part of this underground movement, like I had access to information that the mainstream was hiding from everyone else. I'd spend hours, days, falling down these internet rabbit holes, chasing every lead, every morsel of "truth" that seemed to confirm what I already believed.

And the more I consumed, the more I bought into it. It was like I was building this whole new reality for myself, brick by brick, tweet by tweet, YouTube video by YouTube video. I was constructing my own personal echo chamber, surrounding myself with voices that mirrored my own thoughts and fears back at me.

That's the thing about these echo chambers. They're not just about the information, the so-called facts and figures. They're a whole vibe, a way of seeing the world. Everything gets filtered through this lens of suspicion, where every event and every person is part of some grand conspiracy. And any piece of evidence that doesn't fit that narrative? It gets twisted and warped until it does, or it gets tossed aside, dismissed as part of the cover-up.

I was in deep, real deep. I had cut myself off from anyone who challenged my new worldview, anyone who tried to pull me back to reality. They were all sheep, I thought, blind to the real truth. I was one of the enlightened few, the ones fighting the good fight against the powers that be.

But the longer I stayed in that echo chamber, the more the cracks started to show. Little inconsistencies, predictions that never panned out, smoking gun revelations that turned out to be duds. At first, I found ways to rationalize it, to patch over those cracks with more conspiracy and more denial. But deep down, in a place I didn't want to acknowledge, the doubts were starting to grow.

It's a hell of a thing, confronting the idea that the beliefs you've built your whole identity around might be wrong. It's like staring into the abyss, like facing the void where your sense of self used to be. I didn't want to look, didn't want to admit that I had been duped, that I had bought into a lie. So I clung to those beliefs even harder, retreated even deeper into the comforting womb of the echo chamber.

But the cognitive dissonance, it eats away at you. The constant mental gymnastics you have to do to keep the illusion intact, it wears you down. And the isolation, the alienation from everyone who isn't part of your alternate reality, it's soul-crushing. I was tired, burnt out from the constant state of suspicion and fear, the unending battle against imagined enemies.

And then, one day, something snapped. I had been scrolling through my usual feeds, looking for my next hit of outrage and validation, when I stumbled across a post that made me pause. It was from someone who used to be deep in the same conspiracy circles as me, but who had somehow found their way out. They were talking about their journey, about the moment they realized they were trapped in a hall of mirrors, about the painful process of re-finding themselves and rebuilding their understanding of reality.

Something about their words, their story, it resonated with me in a way I couldn't ignore. It was like a chink of light piercing through the walls of my echo chamber, a glimpse of a world beyond the suspicion and the fear. I felt a flicker of something I hadn't felt in a long time - hope.

That post, it was the start of my own journey out of the rabbit hole. It wasn't a sudden epiphany, more like a slow awakening, a gradual process of untangling myself from the web of lies and delusions I had been caught in for so long. I started to question things I had taken as gospel, started to seek out information from outside my usual bubble.

And it was uncomfortable. It was like learning to see the world anew, like coming out of a long, fevered dream and blinking in the harsh light of day. I had to confront some hard truths about myself, about the way I had been thinking and behaving. I had to face the shame and the guilt of realizing how far I had strayed from reality, how much damage I might have done by spreading disinformation and sowing distrust.

It was humbling, really humbling. I had to learn to be okay with not having all the answers, with admitting when I was wrong. I had to relearn how to engage with people who thought differently than me, how to have actual conversations instead of just shouting matches and name-calling.

But the more I stepped outside my echo chamber, the more I started to see the world in all its messy, complicated glory. I rediscovered the joy of real human connection, of learning from people with diverse experiences and perspectives. I started to appreciate the beauty of nuance, the power of critical thinking and healthy skepticism.

It was like coming back to life, like waking up from a long, cynical slumber. The world wasn't the dark, conspiratorial place I had believed it to be for so long. It was full of shades of gray, full of ordinary people just trying to make sense of it all, just like me.

And as I pieced my worldview back together, as I rebuilt my understanding of truth and reality, I realized that the echo chamber had been a kind of addiction. It had given me a hit of certainty, of righteous anger, of belonging to an in-group that had all the answers. But it was a false high, a cheap substitute for the harder but more rewarding work of engaging with the world as it really is.

Breaking free of that addiction, learning to live in the ambiguity and complexity of reality, it's an ongoing process. There are still moments when I feel the pull of those old thought patterns, when I have to check myself and remember the lessons I've learned. But I'm not going back. I can't. I've seen too much, come too far.

And now, looking back on my time in the echo chamber, I see it for what it was: a trap, a mental prison of my own making. It's a seductive trap, one that preys on our deepest fears and insecurities, our longing for certainty in an uncertain world. But it's a lie, a mirage that can never truly satisfy us.

The truth, the real truth, it's out here in the messy, beautiful chaos of the real world. It's in the stories we share, the connections we forge, the questions we keep asking even when there are no easy answers. It's in the courage to admit when we're wrong, to change our minds, to keep growing and learning and evolving.

That's the trip we're all on, whether we realize it or not. The journey of a lifetime, the search for meaning and truth and connection in a world that's always changing, always challenging us to adapt and expand our understanding.

And the echo chamber? It's just a detour, a wrong turn that can lead us astray if we're not careful. But we always have the power to find our way back, to chart a new course based on reason and empathy and a willingness to engage with the world as it is, not as we wish it to be.

So to anyone out there who might be lost in the labyrinth of disinformation and conspiracy, who might be deep in their own echo chamber, I say this: there is a way out. It's not easy, and it's not comfortable, but it's so worth it. Because the world outside that bubble? It's a trip. A crazy, beautiful, messed-up, awe-inspiring trip. And it's waiting for you, if you're brave enough to step out of the shadows and embrace it.

It's like, we're all on this journey together, even if we're coming at it from different angles, different backgrounds, different belief systems. We're all just trying to make sense of this wild, wonderful, terrifying ride that is life in the 21st century.

And yeah, the internet, social media, all this technology that was supposed to connect us, a lot of times it just ends up driving us apart, locking us in these digital silos where we only hear the echoes of our own opinions bouncing back at us. It's easy to get lost in there, to forget that there's a whole wide world beyond the screen, full of real people with real stories and real struggles.

But that's the thing. We can't let the echo chamber become our whole reality. We've got to remember to step outside of it, to breathe the fresh air of different perspectives, to engage with the world in all its raw, unfiltered glory.

And that's what this journey out of the echo chamber is all about. It's about reclaiming that spirit of authentic experience, about daring to confront the world as it is, warts and all. It's about having the courage to question our own beliefs, to be humble in the face of the vast, unknowable complexity of it all.

Because at the end of the day, none of us have all the answers. We're all just stumbling through this crazy, mixed-up world, trying to make sense of the clues and the cues, trying to find our way to some kind of truth that resonates in our souls.

And the echo chamber? It's a dead end. A cul-de-sac of the mind. It might feel cozy and comforting for a while, but stay in there too long and you start to lose yourself, lose touch with the raw, pulsing reality of life beyond the screen.

So we've got to keep moving, keep exploring, keep opening ourselves up to new experiences and new ways of seeing the world. We've got to be willing to have our minds changed, our hearts expanded, our assumptions challenged.

It's a trip, a never-ending journey into the great unknown. But it's the only journey worth taking, the only way to really live. So let's hit the road and see where it takes us. Let's bust out of our echo chambers and dive headfirst into the swirling, psychedelic wonder of the real world.

It might be a bumpy ride, it might be full of twists and turns and unexpected detours. But that's the beauty of it, the thrill and the terror and the sheer, unbridled adventure of it all.

So let's go. Let's leave the rabbit hole behind and set out on the highway of life, chasing the horizon of truth and meaning and authentic experience. Let's get our kicks, not in the shadowy corners of the internet, but in the bright, blazing sun of the real world waiting just outside our door.

Because in the end, that's where it's at. That's where the real magic happens. Not in the echo chamber, but in the vast, uncharted territories of the mind and the heart and the great wide open. That's where we find ourselves, find each other, find the wild, untamed beauty of this crazy cosmic dance we're all a part of.

So let's ride. Let's break free of our digital prisons and hit the open road of discovery and wonder. The echo chamber's in the rearview now, and the future's unfolding in front of us like a map to the stars. Let's see where it takes us, and who we might become along the way.

3 THE TURNING POINT

The realization that you're lost, that you've been wandering in a maze of mirrors and illusions, it doesn't usually hit you like a lightning bolt. It's more like a slow dawn, a gradual realization as the pieces start to fall into place. For me, that realization came in the form of a breakdown, a moment when the weight of all those doubts and inconsistencies finally came crashing down on me.

I had been walking this path for a long time, getting deeper and deeper into the rabbit hole of conspiracy. But somewhere along the way, I had started to lose myself. The world I had constructed, this alternate reality of secret plots and hidden truths, it had started to feel more real to me than the ground beneath my feet. I had cut myself off from anyone who challenged those beliefs, anyone who tried to pull me back to the surface. I thought I was one of the enlightened few, that I had a sacred duty to spread the truth.

But that truth, it started to unravel. Little by little, the inconsistencies started to pile up. Predictions that never came to pass, revelations that turned out to be smoke and mirrors. At first, I found ways to rationalize it, to patch over the cracks in my belief system. But the doubts kept growing, kept nagging at me.

And then, one day, it all came to a head. I was sitting there, staring at the screen like I had a thousand times before, when something just snapped. The paranoia, the fear, the anger, it all came rushing in like a tidal wave. I couldn't breathe, couldn't think. It was like the walls of my carefully constructed reality were crumbling around me.

In that moment of raw panic, of total breakdown, a strange thing happened. Amidst all the chaos and the fear, a small, still voice emerged. A voice that had been drowned out for so long by the noise of the echo chamber. And it was asking me a question, a question I couldn't ignore: "Is this real? Is this really the truth?"

It was like a spark, a tiny ember of doubt. But as I sat there, shaking and exhausted, that ember started to grow. I started to see my beliefs, my entire worldview, in a new light. Suddenly, it all seemed so flimsy, so insubstantial. The conspiracies, the secret knowledge, it was like a house of cards in a hurricane.

And I realized, with a clarity that was almost painful, that I had been living in a dream world, a fantasy land of my own creation. I had been so hungry for meaning, for purpose, that I had latched onto this alternate reality and let it consume me. But in that moment of breakdown, of total surrender, I saw it for what it was: a prison, a trap that I had built for myself.

It was a shattering realization, one that cut to the core. Everything I had believed, everything I had based my identity on, it was all crumbling away. I felt lost, adrift in a sea of uncertainty. But at the same time, there was a glimmer of something else, something I hadn't felt in a long time: hope.

Because in that moment, I made a choice. A choice to step out of the echo chamber, to walk away from the rabbit hole. A choice to face reality, no matter how painful or uncertain it might be. I didn't know where that path would lead me, didn't know who I would be without my conspiracies. But I knew, with a deep certainty, that I couldn't go back. I had seen the truth, the real truth, and there was no unseeing it.

That choice, it was the hardest thing I've ever done. It meant letting go of everything I had believed, everything that had given my life a sense of meaning and purpose. It meant admitting that I had been wrong, that I had been duped and misled. It meant facing the shame, the guilt, the self-doubt.

But it was also the most liberating thing I've ever done. Because in letting go of those illusions, in stepping out of that echo chamber, I was reclaiming myself. I was choosing to live in the real world, the world of flesh and blood and messy, complicated truth. I was choosing to trust myself, to rebuild my understanding from the ground up.

And so I started walking, started putting one foot in front of the other on this new path. I reached out to people I had pushed away, started seeking out new sources of information and perspectives. It was like learning to walk again, learning to navigate a world that was so much bigger and more complex than the one I had constructed for myself.

There were stumbles, setbacks. Moments when the pull of the old beliefs, the old certainties, was almost too strong to resist. But each time, I reminded myself of that moment of clarity, that flash of truth that had pierced through the fog of delusion. And I kept going, kept pushing forward, even when the path was steep and the way was unclear.

Slowly, painfully, I started to rebuild myself. I started to rediscover the joy of real human connection, the beauty of a world that was messy and complicated and full of shades of gray. I started to find a new sense of purpose, not in some grand conspiracy, but in the simple, daily act of living with reality and integrity.

And as I walked this new path, as I started to come out the other side of that long, dark night of the soul, I realized that I wasn't alone. There were others out there who had been through the same thing, who had found themselves lost in the echo chamber and had made the choice to walk away. We started to find each other, started to build a new community based not on shared delusions, but on a shared commitment to facing reality, no matter how challenging or uncomfortable it might be.

Together, we learned to navigate this new landscape, to support each other on the journey. We shared our stories, our struggles, our triumphs. And slowly, surely, we started to heal, to rebuild our sense of self and our understanding of the world.

It's an ongoing process, this recovery from the rabbit hole. There are still moments of doubt, still times when the old patterns of thinking try to reassert themselves. But now, I have tools I didn't have before. I have a community, a support system. And most of all, I have a deep, unshakeable commitment to the truth, to the world as it really is, not as I want it to be.

Looking back on that turning point, that moment of breakdown that became a breakthrough, I see it now as a gift. A painful, terrifying gift, but a gift nonetheless. Because it forced me to confront myself, to question everything I thought I knew. It shattered my illusions, but it also freed me from a prison I had built for myself.

And now, as I walk this new path, as I continue the lifelong journey of growth and discovery, I feel a sense of gratitude. Gratitude for that moment of grace, of clarity in the midst of chaos. Gratitude for the chance to rebuild, to become more fully myself. And gratitude for the others who walk beside me, who share this commitment to truth and authenticity.

It's not an easy path, this road of truth-seeking. It demands constant vigilance, constant questioning of our own assumptions and biases. It requires the courage to stand up to the lies and the manipulation, even when they come from within our own minds. It takes a willingness to be wrong, to change our minds in the face of new evidence.

But it's a path worth walking, a journey worth taking. Because in the end, it's the only way to find real meaning, real connection. It's the only way to be truly free.

And so we keep walking, keep putting one foot in front of the other. We lean on each other when the path gets steep, we celebrate each other's victories and mourn each other's losses. We are truth-seekers, reality-facers. We have been to the bottom of the rabbit hole and back again, and we know the value of the light.

The turning point is behind us now, receding in the rearview mirror. But the journey, the adventure, the quest for understanding - that stretches out before us, a road winding into the horizon. We don't know where it will take us, don't know what challenges and joys lie ahead. But we know that we will walk it together, hand in hand and heart to heart.

And we know that every step, every stumble, every moment of doubt and discovery, is a chance to learn, to grow, to become more fully ourselves. We are explorers of the real, cartographers of the human experience in all its messy, complicated beauty.

The echo chamber, the rabbit hole, they are behind us now. Fading memories of a long, strange trip. But the lessons we learned there, the strength we found in breaking free - those we carry with us, lodestones to guide us on our way.

And so we walk on, into the great wide open of possibility. We embrace the mystery, the uncertainty, the endless unfolding of a world that is always new, always waiting to be discovered. We are the ones who have seen outside the rabbit hole, and we have chosen to live in the light.

Let the journey continue, let the adventure unfold. We are ready, hand in hand and heart to heart. The turning point has come, and a new chapter begins. Let us fill its pages with courage, with wonder, with the fierce and joyful pursuit of truth. The road awaits, and we are the ones we have been waiting for.

There is a saying among travelers, among those who walk the winding paths of the world: the journey is the destination. And for us, the journey is one of truth-seeking, of reality-facing. It is a journey that will last a lifetime, a quest that will take us to the far horizons of the mind and the soul.

But we are not daunted by the distance, not discouraged by the difficulties. For we have known the depths, the darkness of the rabbit hole. And we have chosen the light, chosen the hard and joyful work of living in the real world, in all its complexity and contradiction.

We are the ones who have turned the corner, who have faced our fears and our doubts and our delusions head-on. We have looked into the abyss, and we have chosen to build a bridge across it, a bridge of truth and trust and connection.

And as we walk this bridge, as we make our way step by step into the unknown, we find that we are not alone. There are others out there, other travelers on this path of awakening. We see them in the distance, their lights twinkling like stars in the night sky. And we know that we are part of a constellation, a network of reality seekers spanning the globe and the generations.

This knowledge, this sense of connection, it gives us strength when the way is hard. It reminds us that we are part of something larger, something deeper. A human story that has always been about the search for meaning, for purpose, for that which sets us free.

And so we keep walking, keep shining our lights into the darkness. We share our stories, our struggles, our triumphs. We build new maps, new ways of navigating this strange and wondrous world.
We are the weavers of a new reality, a reality based not on fear and lies

and hidden agendas, but on courage and compassion and the deep knowing that we are all in this together. We are the ones who have chosen to wake up, to grow up, to show up for the hard and necessary work of healing ourselves and our world.

And as we walk this path, as we make our way through the twists and turns of this great adventure, we find that the turning point, the moment of breakthrough, is not a one-time event. It is a choice we make every day, every moment. A choice to face reality, to speak truth, to live with authenticity and integrity.

It is not always easy, this choice. There are times when the pull of the old stories, the old patterns, is strong. Times when we are tempted to retreat back into the comfort of the known, the familiar.

But we have tasted freedom, have touched the truth that lies beyond the veil of illusion. And we can never go back, never unsee what we have seen. We are the ones who have been to the mountaintop, and we know that the view from the summit is worth the climb.

And so we keep climbing, keep reaching for that higher ground. We fall, we stumble, we get back up again. We learn from our mistakes, we forgive ourselves and each other. We make amends, we make a difference.

This is the turning point, this is the moment when we choose to become the authors of our own story, the creators of our own reality. We are the ones we have been waiting for, the heroes of our own epic tale.

Let the journey continue, let the adventure unfold. We are ready, hand in hand and heart to heart. The turning point has come, and a new world awaits. Let us build it together, brick by brick and dream by dream. The road is long, but the destination is worth the journey. And we are the ones who will make it so.

4 DETOXING FROM DIGITAL

So there I was, standing at the edge, the rabbit hole yawning behind me and the wide, wild world of reality stretching out ahead. I knew I wanted to leave that echo chamber behind, to step into the light of truth and clarity. But the question that hit me, the one that nearly knocked me off my feet, was: how? How do you untangle yourself from a web of disinformation that's woven itself into every corner of your life, your mind, your very sense of self?

It wasn't going to be a simple snip of the scissors, I knew that much. The tendrils of conspiracy and alternative facts, they had burrowed deep, wrapping themselves around my thought patterns, my daily habits, my relationships. Extracting myself from that labyrinth, it was going to take more than just a snap decision. It was going to require serious effort, a strategic game plan, and a whole heap of patience and compassion for myself.

The first step, the one that seemed most obvious and most daunting all at once, was to cut off the constant drip-feed of disinformation that had been my mental sustenance for so long. That meant taking a long, unflinching look at my media diet, at all the ways I was letting the rabbit hole seep into my brain on a daily basis. I sat down and really examined it, mapping out the social media accounts I followed, the YouTube rabbit holes I regularly tumbled down, the websites I checked compulsively throughout the day. Each one of these, I realized with a sinking feeling, was a potential pipeline straight from the heart of the echo chamber.

But knowledge is power, or so they say. And armed with this clear-eyed understanding of my digital habits, I knew I could start to make some changes. It was time for a serious detox, a purge of all the sources that were keeping me tethered to the world of alternative facts. I started hitting that unfollow button with a vengeance, muting keywords that always seemed to dredge up the most fringe content, even installing extensions on my browser to block certain sites entirely. It felt strange at first, almost like I was cutting off a part of myself, amputating a limb that had become so familiar I hardly noticed it anymore. But as the days ticked by and the fog began to lift, I started to notice a lightness in my mental load, a new spaciousness in my thoughts. Without the constant barrage of doomsday predictions and us-versus-them rhetoric, my mind finally had room to breathe, to stretch, to consider new angles and perspectives.

But detoxing from digital, I quickly realized, wasn't just about cutting out the negative. It was also about actively seeking out healthier fare, about curating a media diet that would nourish my mind and soul in the way the echo chamber never could. I started making a conscious effort to diversify my information intake, following accounts and publications that tackled complex topics with nuance and hard facts instead of knee-jerk outrage. I sought out voices that challenged my assumptions in constructive ways, that modeled the kind of critical thinking and good-faith discussion I wanted to cultivate in myself. It was like learning to eat my vegetables after a lifetime of subsisting on junk food - not always easy, not always immediately satisfying, but so much better for me in the long run.

As I started to rebuild my media landscape from the ground up, I could feel my mind beginning to change, to adapt to this new way of engaging with information. But I knew that truly breaking free from the echo chamber was going to require more than just a shift in what I consumed. It was going to require a fundamental rewiring of how I processed and interacted with information, period. All those knee-jerk, emotionally-driven habits of thought that the rabbit hole had nurtured, the ones that had me reaching for the share button before my rational brain could even catch up - they needed to be replaced with slower, more intentional approaches.

One of the strategies that really helped me in this rewiring process was what I started calling "information clarity" - basically, a set of mental checks and balances I would run through before letting a new piece of information fully sink into my brain. It meant things like always looking for corroborating sources, considering the potential biases and agendas at play, and most importantly, questioning my own immediate gut reactions to a piece of content. Was I latching onto this information because it confirmed what I already believed, or because it was actually well-supported by facts? Was I dismissing it out of hand because it challenged my preconceptions, or because it truly lacked credibility? Learning to ask these questions, to build that split-second habit of pausing and assessing before internalizing, it was like building a mental immune system against disinformation.

But as much as I was learning to think differently in this new post-rabbit hole reality, I was also having to learn to feel differently. Because the truth is, extricating yourself from an echo chamber isn't just a cognitive process. It's a deeply emotional one too, and those emotional ripple effects can linger long after your beliefs have shifted. The sense of certainty and belonging that had come with my conspiracy worldview, the feeling of being one of the select few who knew the "real" truth - letting go of that was hard, even as I recognized how illusory it had always been. There was a very real grief in saying goodbye to the person I had been in the rabbit hole, in watching that identity crumble away, even if I knew it had been built on a foundation of sand all along.

To navigate this rocky emotional terrain, I had to learn to extend myself a whole lot of grace and compassion. I leaned into practices of mindfulness, learning to observe my thoughts and feelings without immediately attaching to them or being swallowed up by them. When the old anxiety or paranoia would start to creep in, I practiced recognizing it, naming it, even thanking it for trying to keep me safe in its own misguided way - and then gently redirecting my mind to the present, to what was real and true in the moment. I sought out the support of a therapist who helped me process the complicated knot of emotions that came with this kind of major worldview shift - the grief, the anger, the fear, the overwhelming uncertainty of it all. Slowly, session by session, I began to build a new sense of self - one rooted not in the false certainties of conspiratorial thinking, but in the ever-unfolding, ever-questioning process of growth and understanding.

There were times, of course, when I would stumble, when the siren song of the rabbit hole would grow loud again and I'd feel the tug of those old beliefs, those old patterns of thinking. Moments when the sheer complexity and ambiguity of reality felt too heavy to bear, and I'd long for the false comfort of a world divided neatly into good and evil, us and them. But each time I weathered one of these crises without giving in, each time I chose the harder path of nuance and ambiguity over the easy certainty of the echo chamber, I could feel myself growing stronger, more rooted in my commitment to truth over comfort.

And slowly, one day at a time, one small success building on the last, I started to find my footing in this new reality. I started to rediscover the joy of learning for its own sake, of following my curiosity down new and winding paths without needing to know exactly where they would lead. I started to build new relationships, finding community not in the false kinship of conspiracy but in the honest, messy work of trying to understand the world and each other a little better. The rabbit hole, I realized, had been a labyrinth of mirrors, reflecting my own fears and biases back at me endlessly. But the world outside of it, the world of verifiable facts and multiple perspectives and irreducible complexity - that was the real terra incognito, ripe for true exploration and discovery.

Looking back, I can see that my strategies for digital detox, all those little day-to-day habits of media consumption and critical analysis, were really just the outward manifestation of a much deeper shift, an inner reorientation toward reality in all its many-textured splendor. The real work of disengagement, I've come to understand, isn't just about cutting ties with toxic information sources or even about learning to think more critically, essential as those things are. It's about fundamentally changing your relationship to truth, to the process of trying to make sense of the world around you. It's about learning to live in the questions, in the space of not-knowing, and finding the courage to keep moving forward even when the path ahead is foggy and uncertain.

That kind of shift, that kind of deep rewiring - it's not a one-and-done kind of thing. Even now, all these months and years after taking those first shaky steps out of the rabbit hole, I still find myself having to recommit to it, again and again, with every new piece of information I encounter, every new challenge to my understanding that arises. The old habits of mind, the old yearnings for certainty and simplicity, they don't just disappear overnight. Learning to engage with reality on its own wild, unruly terms - it's a practice, a discipline, a lifelong journey of growth and discovery.

But it's a journey that's given me gifts beyond measure, that's opened up my world in ways I never could have imagined from inside the echo chamber. The freedom that comes from liberating your mind from the shackles of disinformation, from learning to trust your own ability to seek out and weigh the evidence, to think for yourself even in the face of complexity and uncertainty - it's the kind of freedom that can't be taken away from you, no matter what new conspiracy or moral panic comes down the pike. And the relationships, the sense of real community that comes from engaging with others in a spirit of honest inquiry and shared humanity, instead of paranoia and polarization - that's the kind of nourishment that can sustain a soul through the darkest of times.

So if there's anyone out there reading this who's still lost in the labyrinth of the rabbit hole, anyone who's feeling that first tug of doubt, that first longing to find a way out - know that you're not alone, and you're not crazy for wanting to leave. The journey ahead of you may be hard, it may be scary, it may require you to let go of some things that have felt like lifelines in the past. But I promise you, from the bottom of my heart, that it's so, so worth it.

There's a world of wonders waiting for you on the other side, a reality so much richer and more multifaceted than any conspiracy theory could ever dream of offering. All you have to do is take that first step, and keep on walking, one day at a time, towards the light of your own understanding. The road will rise up to meet you, and you'll find that you're stronger than you ever knew. Just keep going, keep questioning, keep daring to imagine a different way of being. I'll be rooting for you, every step of the way.

5 REBUILDING REALITY

As the fog of the echo chamber started to lift, as the digital detox began to work its magic, I found myself blinking in the harsh light of a strange new landscape. It was like coming out of a long dream, the kind that feels so real you're not sure what to believe when you finally wake up. The world I had constructed for myself, the alternate reality I had inhabited for so long - it was lying in pieces all around me, shattered fragments of conspiracy theories and fringe ideas that didn't seem to hold the same weight anymore. But if these weren't my truth anymore, if this wasn't the solid ground I had thought I was standing on - then what was?

How do you rebuild your entire sense of reality from scratch?

This was the question that haunted me as I took those first shaky steps into the next phase of my journey out of the rabbit hole. Having purged myself of the constant stream of disinformation, having created that space in my mind for something new to grow, I was now faced with the daunting task of actually filling it. Of constructing a new understanding of the world, a new framework for making sense of everything that had once seemed so clear and certain. But this time, I knew, I couldn't rely on the seductive false comforts of the echo chamber. This time, I had to build my reality on the solid bedrock of empirical truth, no matter how challenging or uncomfortable that might be.

The first step in this process, I quickly realized, was a complete and total inversion of how I had been approaching information for so long. In the depths of the rabbit hole, I had been operating on pure confirmation bias - seeking out only the content that validated what I already believed, that reinforced my preexisting narratives, and dismissing anything that dared to challenge or contradict them. It was like I had been walking through the world with blinders on, only seeing what I wanted to see, what I needed to see to keep my fractured worldview intact.

But now, as I started to rebuild, I knew I had to rip those blinders off. I had to make a conscious, concerted effort to flip that script entirely, to actively seek out information that challenged my assumptions and introduced new perspectives. This was deeply uncomfortable at first, almost physically painful. It's never easy to admit that you might be wrong about something, especially something as core to your identity as your beliefs about how the world works. Opening myself up to that possibility, to the idea that the cherished convictions I had built my life around might not actually line up with reality - it felt like tearing open a wound, exposing the rawest, most vulnerable parts of myself to the harsh light of day.

But as much as it hurt, as much as every fiber of my being seemed to resist it, I knew it was necessary. I knew that if I really wanted to build my understanding on a foundation of truth, I had to be willing to question everything, to hold all my ideas up to the light of empirical scrutiny. So I dove in headfirst. I started engaging with a much wider range of sources, prioritizing the ones I knew I could trust - reputable news outlets, peer-reviewed scientific journals, in-depth analyses from recognized experts in their fields. I challenged myself to read things that made me uncomfortable, that poked holes in my long-held assumptions and forced me to think harder, to grapple with complexity and nuance in a way I never had before.

Slowly but surely, through this process of active, critical engagement, I started to piece together a new picture of the world. And the more I explored, the more I learned, the more I realized just how much I had been missing, how much had been hidden from view in the narrow confines of the echo chamber. The world, I was starting to understand, was not the simple, black-and-white place I had imagined it to be. It was a tapestry of interwoven shades of gray, a complex dance of cause and effect, of competing forces and perspectives and interests. There were rarely simple answers or tidy explanations, rarely heroes and villains in the stark terms I had once clung to.

This realization, this dawning comprehension of just how messy and multifaceted reality really was - it was both liberating and terrifying all at once. On one hand, it was a relief to feel like I was finally seeing the world as it truly was, not as I wanted or needed it to be. There was a kind of freedom in that, a sense of empowerment that came from facing facts head-on, from trusting in my own ability to navigate complexity and ambiguity. But at the same time, letting go of those false certainties, those comforting narratives that had made everything seem so clear-cut and comprehensible - it was profoundly destabilizing, like the ground itself was shifting under my feet.

Because the truth is, rebuilding your reality from the ground up isn't just an intellectual exercise. It's not just about swapping out one set of beliefs for another, updating your mental software with the latest patches and fixes. It's a deeply emotional, existential process, one that strikes at the very core of who you think you are and how you make sense of your place in the universe. The fantasies of the echo chamber, the grand conspiracies and secrets- as twisted as they were, they had also served a purpose. They had injected a sense of order and meaning into a world that often feels chaotic and random, that rarely conforms to our deepest yearnings for justice and clarity. They had provided a reassuring framework, a way to numb the existential dread and anomie that come from staring too long into the abyss of an indifferent universe.

So in letting go of those fantasies, in facing the often painful complexities of the real world head-on, I found myself grappling with some of the rawest, most primal fears and anxieties of the human condition. The fear of meaninglessness, of being adrift in a cosmos that has no inherent purpose or plan. The dread of powerlessness, of being at the mercy of forces and systems too vast and entrenched for any one person to change. The vertiginous sensation of uncertainty, of realizing just how little we can ever truly know or control. These were the specters that had always lurked beneath the surface of my conspiratorial worldview, the dark tides that the false certainties of the rabbit hole had helped keep at bay.

Now, as I struggled to rebuild my reality on a sturdier foundation, I found myself having to confront those specters head-on. I had to learn to sit with the discomfort they evoked, to stare into the face of existential anxiety without flinching or reaching for easy answers. I had to develop new sources of meaning and resilience, new ways of making sense of my place in a world that often defies sense-making. It was a process of soul-searching and self-discovery as much as it was one of intellectual growth, a journey into the deepest, most uncharted regions of my own psyche.

To navigate this inner landscape, I had to cultivate a whole new set of emotional tools and practices. I delved into the worlds of mindfulness and meditation, learning to observe my own thoughts and feelings with a kind of gentle, nonjudgmental awareness. When the old anxieties would arise, when I'd feel the tug of those well-worn grooves of conspiratorial thinking, I practiced sitting with those sensations, breathing into them, letting them pass through me like waves rather than getting sucked under by their undertow. I sought out communities of support, spaces where I could process the challenges of this transformation in the company of others who were committed to living in truth, no matter how uncomfortable or complex that truth might be.

And slowly, painstakingly, through a thousand tiny acts of courage and self-compassion, I began to build a new sense of identity and purpose for myself. One that was rooted not in the false certainties and illusory belonging of the echo chamber, but in the more grounded, hard-won satisfactions of engaging authentically with the real world in all its unruly complexity. I found a kind of meaning in the small, daily rituals of truth-seeking and truth-telling, in the constant effort to align my beliefs with empirical reality, no matter where that journey took me. I discovered a sense of connection and solidarity not in the paranoid "us vs. them" of conspiracy thinking, but in the recognition of our shared humanity, our shared struggles to make sense of a world that often defies easy sense-making.

This process of rebuilding my reality, of reconstructing my entire worldview from the ground up - it's still very much a work in progress, even now. There are still moments when the old habits of mind reassert themselves, when I feel the siren call of those false certainties beckoning from the depths of the rabbit hole. There are still times when the sheer magnitude of the world's complexity, the seeming intractability of its problems and injustices, threatens to overwhelm me, to send me spiraling back into the comforting delusions of conspiratorial thinking.

But with each of those moments weathered, each temptation resisted, I find my footing on the path of truth-seeking growing a little surer, a little steadier. Each time I choose to embrace reality in all its difficult, uncomfortable messiness - to follow the facts where they lead, even when they lead me away from what I thought I knew - I feel a tiny bit more liberated from the shackles of self-deception, a tiny bit more alive to the wondrous, terrible, endlessly fascinating world as it actually is.

And that, I'm coming to understand, is the real gift of this whole journey. Not some final, fixed understanding of the world, not some stable, unchanging sense of certainty - but rather the continuous, lifelong process of discovery itself, the commitment to living in alignment with reality, no matter how challenging or disorienting that may be. In learning to engage with the world on its own terms, to accept the fundamental groundlessness and uncertainty of the human condition, I'm tapping into a source of meaning and aliveness that runs so much deeper than the false comforts of the echo chamber ever could.

It's not an easy path, this road of radical truth-seeking. It demands a kind of existential courage, a willingness to stare into the face of the unknown, to build and rebuild your reality in an ongoing process of growth and transformation. It requires a deep humility, a recognition of just how little we can ever truly know or control. But it also opens up possibilities for connection and discovery and self-actualization that I never could have imagined from the depths of the rabbit hole.

In the end, I'm coming to believe, this process of continually shedding delusions and realigning myself with empirical reality - it's not just a way of making sense of the world. It's a way of radically embracing the miracle of my own existence, of marveling at the sheer improbability and preciousness of being alive and aware in a universe as vast and strange and endlessly surprising as this one. And that, I suspect, is a kind of truth worth building an entire life around - a reality more vivid and urgent and sacred than any conspiracy theory could ever touch.

The road stretches on ahead of me, winding and uncertain as it may be. But I know now that I'd rather walk that path, with all its challenges and discomforts and moments of existential vertigo, than ever again lose myself in the false comforts of delusion. Reality, in all its unruly complexity and beauty and heartbreak, is the only ground I want to stand on. And I'm only just beginning to discover the wonders and possibilities that open up when you really, truly commit to seeing it as it is. It's a wild ride, a dizzying dance on the knife's edge of uncertainty - but I wouldn't trade it for anything. Because to be fully awake, fully alive to the truth of the world and of your own being - that, I'm beginning to suspect, is what this strange and fleeting thing called life is really all about.

6 MIND OVER MATTER

As I kept trucking down this road out of the rabbit hole, as the miles of mental landscape stretched out behind me, I started to feel a shift happening deep down. It wasn't just about how I was understanding the world anymore, not just about the ideas and the theories and the facts that I was using to navigate. No, this was something else entirely, something that was changing the very tint and texture of my experience, the emotional hum of my day-to-day reality.

You see, for so long, living in that echo chamber, my mind had been stuck in this constant state of fever pitch. It was like I was perpetually braced for impact, my nervous system dialed up to eleven, always scanning the horizon for the next catastrophe, the next grand conspiracy, the next existential threat. That anxiety, that sense of impending doom - it had become my baseline, my normal. I'd almost forgotten what it felt like to inhabit my own mind without that crackle of fear, that background radiation of suspicion.

But now, as I kept putting one foot in front of the other on this path of digital detox and reality rebuilding, I could feel something starting to ease, to unfurl, to open up inside of me. That chronic state of fight-or-flight, that sense of the walls always closing in - it was starting to lift, bit by bit. And in its place, a budding sense of spaciousness, of equilibrium. It was like I was rediscovering a version of myself that I had lost somewhere along the way, a me that could move through the world with a little more grace, a little more groundedness.

This shift in my mental landscape, it caught me by surprise at first. I had been so fixated on the external process of extracting myself from the rabbit hole - on curating my media diet and fact-checking my assumptions and all that good stuff - that I hadn't really stopped to consider how it might be transforming my inner life. But here it was, this unlooked-for gift, this quiet revolution of the psyche. The further I got from the fog of disinformation and delusion, the more I could feel my mind beginning to clear, like a sky after a storm. The obsessive thought loops, the knee-jerk reactivity, the constant sense of being under siege - it was all starting to ease, to give way to something new.

And the more I leaned into this shift, the more I started to see it as an integral part of the journey I was on. It wasn't just about rearranging the furniture of my beliefs, about swapping out one set of ideas for another. No, this was about fundamentally rewiring my relationship to reality, about learning to engage with the world not through a lens of fear and fantasy, but with a grounded sense of presence, of clear-eyed curiosity.

Of course, it wasn't like flipping a switch. This kind of deep rewiring, it's a process, a practice. It requires a certain intentionality, a commitment to showing up day after day to the work of reclaiming your mind from the clutches of anxiety and delusion. For me, a big part of that work has been about cultivating a new relationship with the present moment, about learning to anchor my awareness in the here and now rather than getting swept away by the tides of rumination and projection.

Mindfulness, meditation, call it what you will - these practices have become my North Star, my way of navigating the choppy waters of the mind. Every day, I carve out a little time to just sit and breathe, to observe the comings and goings of my thoughts without getting hooked by them. And every day, I try to bring that same quality of presence, of non-judgmental awareness to my encounters with the world beyond. When I feel myself starting to spiral into worst-case scenarios or latch onto a juicy bit of conspiratorial thinking, I try to catch it, to meet it with a bit of gentle curiosity rather than running with it down the rabbit hole.

It's not always easy, this practice of mental clarity. The grooves of anxious and delusional thinking, they run deep, carved into the soft tissue of my brain by years of repetition. There are still plenty of times when I find myself slipping into old patterns, when the siren song of certainty and suspicion starts to sound mighty tempting. But with each passing day, each moment of choosing presence over panic, I can feel those grooves starting to soften, to lose their grip.

And as they do, as I keep leaning into this practice of radical presence, I'm discovering a capacity for joy, for wonder, for deep connection that I never knew I had. It's like, when you're not constantly bracing for the apocalypse, when your mind isn't perpetually hijacked by phantoms and phantasms, there's so much more room for the good stuff, for the richness and beauty that's always right here, right in front of our faces.

I find myself savoring the small pleasures that I used to barrel past in my rush to the next doom scroll - the way the light slants through the trees on my morning walk, the sound of a friend's laughter, the simple animal comfort of a good meal or a warm bed. I'm learning to meet challenges and uncertainties not with a white-knuckle grip, but with a kind of open-handed curiosity, a willingness to sit with discomfort and ambiguity without needing to resolve it into some kind of grand conspiracy.

And perhaps most transformatively, I'm rediscovering the joys of real human connection, of building relationships based on authenticity and vulnerability rather than shared fear and delusion. During my time in the rabbit hole, I had become so isolated, so cut off from any kind of genuine intimacy. My interactions, even with people I ostensibly cared about, had taken on this transactional quality - less about seeing and being seen and more about comparing notes on the latest world-ending prophecy.

But now, as I keep practicing showing up as I am, without the mask of suspicion or the need to proselytize, I'm starting to remember what it feels like to truly connect, to let myself be touched and transformed by the miracle of other human beings. I'm learning to be vulnerable, to share my doubts and my struggles as well as my joys and my triumphs. And in that vulnerability, that willingness to be seen in all my imperfect humanity, I'm finding a sense of belonging, of interdependence that runs so much deeper than any conspiracy-fueled bond ever could.

This is the real alchemy of the journey I'm on, the true gold at the end of the rainbow. Not just a new set of beliefs, but a new way of being in the world, a new relationship to my own mind and heart and to the vast, vibrant web of life that surrounds me. It's a constant practice, a daily choice to keep stepping into the unknown, to keep leaning into reality in all its unruly beauty and complexity.

There are still moments, of course, when the pull of the rabbit hole reasserts itself, when I feel the tug of those old stories, those old habits of mind. Moments when the sheer weight of the world's suffering, the intractability of its problems and injustices, starts to feel like too much to bear, when the fantasy of a simple explanation, a grand unified theory of everything starts to beckon.

But more and more, I'm learning to meet those moments with compassion, with a kind of fierce and tender presence. To hold myself in the state of uncertainty without needing to escape into the false comfort of a fixed belief or a final answer. To trust in my own capacity to keep showing up, to keep practicing, to keep walking this path of radical presence and perpetual transformation.

And as I do, as I keep putting one foot in front of the other on this road to somewhere freer and truer and more beautifully human, I can feel the landscape of my mind continuing to change, to open up in ways I never could have imagined from the depths of the rabbit hole. The anxieties and obsessions that once felt so solid, so immovable - they're starting to take on a kind of gossamer quality, like wisps of mist burning off in the morning sun of awareness.

In their place, a growing sense of spaciousness, of possibility. A feeling of being at home in the vastness of a universe that's so much stranger and more sacred than any conspiracy theory could ever capture. A deep, abiding sense of gratitude for the sheer fact of being here, of getting to participate in this grand, gorgeously messy dance of life in all its heartbreak and in all its grace.

This is the real adventure, the ultimate trip. Not some fever-dream of secrets and hidden agendas, but the raw, unfiltered encounter with reality itself, in all its terror and in all its wonder. It's not a journey for the faint of heart, not a path for those who need the false comfort of easy answers and final destinations.

But for those with the courage to keep walking, to keep leaning into the beautiful, broken open mystery of it all - there are rewards beyond measure, treasures hidden in the very dirt and disorder of the daily grind. There is a kind of liberation that comes from letting go of the need to know, from trading the prison of certainty for the wide open skies of pure, unmediated presence.

And there is, I am coming to believe, a kind of quiet revolution in the act of showing up like this, in the daily practice of choosing reality over reassurance, of meeting the world with an open heart and an unwavering commitment to the true. It's a revolution that starts in the secret corners of our own minds, in the moment-to-moment choices we make about what to feed and what to starve, what to cling to and what to let go.

But from those small choices, those tiny acts of integrity and courage - whole worlds can change, whole constellations of human possibility can start to shine. We may never know the full ripple effects of our own personal journey out of the rabbit hole, the ways in which our hard-won presence and clarity might touch and transform the lives of others.

But I have a feeling, a hunch, that every single one of us who makes this voyage, who dares to let go of delusion and keep facing into the raw, beautiful truth of the real - we're part of something bigger, something vaster and more consequential than we can possibly imagine. We're part of a great remembering, a collective realization of the simple, sacred fact of our own existence, our own inextricable place in the web of life.

And that, my friends - that's the real conspiracy, the only one that matters in the end. The conspiracy of presence, of reality, of showing up fully to the miracle of each moment, each irreplaceable encounter with the mystery. It's a conspiracy that anyone can join, a rabbit hole that leads not into darkness and isolation, but into the fierce, tender light of our own shared humanity.

So here's to the journey, to the long and winding road out of illusion and into the raw, resplendent real. Here's to the courage to keep walking, to keep practicing, to keep leaning into the beautiful, broken open mystery of it all. And here's to the conspiracy of presence, the quiet revolution of showing up, moment after moment, to the vast, vibrant miracle of life itself.

May we all find our way home to that place, that space of clear-eyed wonder and open-hearted presence. May we all remember the truth of who and what we really are, beneath the noise and the static of delusion. And may we all conspire, in ways great and small, to keep bringing that truth, that presence, that fierce and tender love - to keep bringing it all the way into the astonishing world.

7 A NEW DAWN

As I kept moving forward on this journey out of the rabbit hole, as the miles of mental and emotional terrain unfolded behind me, I started to feel a shift happening that was deeper than deep, more profound than anything I'd yet encountered. It wasn't just about the changes happening inside my own head anymore, the rewiring of my own mental pathways. No, this was something that was spilling out into the world beyond, transforming the very shape and texture of my life on the most fundamental levels.

You see, when you've been living in the echo chamber for as long as I had, when you've made the pursuit of conspiracy your primary mission, your raison d'être - it starts to consume you in ways that go beyond just the intellectual. It becomes the organizing principle of your existence, the magnetic north to which all your energies and attentions are constantly calibrated. Every moment of every day is oriented around this grand quest for hidden truth, this battle against the forces of deception and control.

But now, as I kept walking this path of digital detox and mental emancipation, as I kept untangling myself from the web of suspicion and delusion - I was starting to discover just how much of my life had been hijacked by the rabbit hole, just how much of my time and my passion and my very sense of self had been swallowed up by the echo chamber. It was like I was waking up from a long dream, blinking in the harsh light of a reality that was at once utterly familiar and strangely, dizzyingly new.

Suddenly, I found myself with all these vast expanses of mental and emotional bandwidth that had once been monopolized by the pursuit of conspiracy. Hours upon hours that I used to spend hunched over my screen, manically consuming and regurgitating the latest theories - they were now stretching out before me like some kind of uncharted territory, a wilderness of possibility that I was only just beginning to map.

At first, I'll be real with you, this newfound spaciousness was straight-up terrifying. It was like stepping out of a cramped, cluttered room that you've been living in for years and finding yourself in the middle of a wide-open field, the horizon stretching out in every direction with no landmarks in sight. I felt disoriented, unmoored, like I'd lost the very coordinates by which I'd been navigating my existence for so long.

I mean, who was I, if not a warrior for truth, a lone crusader against the machinations of deep conspiracy? What was my purpose, my mission, if not to unravel the grand conspiratorial web that I'd convinced myself was lurking behind every headline, every global event? Without the constant adrenaline drip of the echo chamber, without the sense of righteous urgency that had propelled me through my days - I felt like a pilot who'd suddenly lost sight of the horizon, flying blind into some unknown void.

But as I kept moving forward, as I leaned into the discomfort and the vertigo of this new existential terrain - I started to realize that the void was anything but empty. In fact, it was brimming with a richness and a vitality that I had been missing out on for so long, a whole universe of experience and connection and meaning that had been hidden from me by the blinders of the rabbit hole.

Freed from the compulsive gravitational pull of the screen, I found myself reconnecting with all these parts of myself and my life that had been languishing in the shadows, starved of attention and nourishment. I rediscovered the simple, profound joy of losing myself in a good book, of letting the words wash over me and transport me to new worlds without the constant itch to fact-check or decode. I started taking long, rambling walks in nature, letting my feet and my thoughts wander where they would, without the need to constantly document or dissect or share.

I even dusted off some old hobbies and interests that I hadn't touched in years, things like strumming on my beat-up old bike or puttering around in the garden, getting my hands dirty in the soil and watching tiny green shoots push their way towards the sun. And as I engaged more and more with these simple, embodied pleasures, as I let myself get lost in the flow of creation and play and curiosity - I started to feel a new sense of identity taking root, a sense of self that was grounded not in the abstract pursuits of the mind, but in the concrete, sensual realities of the world around me.

Slowly but surely, I was learning to derive a sense of meaning and purpose not from being a warrior for truth, but from the tangible contributions I was making to the ecosystem of my own existence - from the meals I was cooking and sharing with friends, from the seeds I was planting and tending in the earth. I was discovering that there was a deep, sustaining satisfaction in creating something real, something that existed beyond the ephemeral buzz of the online world - a satisfaction that the rabbit hole, for all its intensity and intrigue, could never provide.

And nowhere was this shift more palpable, more transformative, than in my relationships with other human beings. Because the thing about living in the rabbit hole, about making conspiracy your primary lens for interacting with the world - is that it warps the very fabric of your connections with others, distorts the delicate web of empathy and understanding that binds us together as social creatures.

When you're always looking for hidden agendas, always parsing every interaction for signs of deception or manipulation - it becomes almost impossible to truly see the person in front of you, to connect with them on a level that goes beyond the surface of ideology or belief. Your conversations become these charged, frenetic exchanges, more about scoring points and converting the unconverted than about any kind of genuine dialogue or discovery.

But now, as I continued to shed the distorting filters of conspiratorial thinking, as I learned to engage with the world on its own messy, multifaceted terms - I was starting to remember what it felt like to really be with another human being, to listen and share and explore without agenda, without the need to constantly defend or persuade. I found myself having these conversations of incredible depth and nuance, these free-flowing, jazz-like exchanges where we would riff off each other's ideas and experiences, following the thread of curiosity wherever it might lead.

I was learning to see the people in my life not as potential allies or adversaries in some grand ideological battle, but as complex, irreducible individuals, each with their own unique stories and struggles and hopes and fears. And in opening myself up to the full spectrum of their humanity, in letting myself be touched and transformed by the raw, unfiltered reality of another consciousness brushing up against my own - I was discovering a sense of connection, of intimacy, that was light-years beyond anything I had ever experienced in the echo chamber.

This renewed capacity for authentic relation, for seeing and being seen - it started to ripple out into every corner of my life, infusing even the most mundane interactions with a sense of vitality and meaning. I found myself striking up conversations with strangers in the grocery store checkout line, swapping recipes and gardening tips with my elderly neighbor. Everywhere I went, I felt this new sense of permeability, this openness to the world and all its inhabitants that had been so long occluded by the paranoid insularity of the rabbit hole.

And the more I leaned into this newfound embodiment, the more I said yes to the myriad invitations to engagement and connection that the world was constantly extending - the more I felt my life opening up in ways I never could have imagined, expanding outward in concentric circles of community and care and co-creation.

I started getting involved in local projects and initiatives, lending my skills and my energy to causes that I cared about not because I thought they were part of some grand conspiratorial endgame, but because they mattered to the real people and places that I had come to love. I found myself forging deep, nourishing friendships, the kind built not on shared suspicion but on shared presence, shared laughter, shared tears.

And through it all I could feel myself coming back to life in the most profound sense - not just intellectually or emotionally, but spiritually, existentially. It was like I was remembering, on a deep level, what it meant to be a part of something larger than myself, to be woven into the grand, sprawling tapestry of life on this planet in all its unruly beauty and heartbreak.

Because the thing is, when you're trapped in the echo chamber, when your whole reality is filtered through the lens of conspiracy and fear - it's so easy to lose sight of that fundamental truth, that bedrock sense of belonging to the world. You start to see yourself as separate, as special, as one of the chosen few who can see through the veil of illusion to the sinister machinations behind the scenes. And in that separateness, that cosmic loneliness - it becomes almost impossible to feel the innate kinship, the radical interdependence that is our birthright as living beings.

But out here, beyond the rabbit hole - that kinship, that interdependence, is impossible to ignore. It's in the very air we breathe, the ground beneath our feet, the food on our plates and the friends at our tables. It's in the vast, intricate web of relationships and reciprocities that sustains us, that nourishes us, that gives our lives meaning and purpose and place.

And the more I attune myself to that web, the more I let myself be held and humbled and transformed by it - the more I feel a sense of wholeness, of homecoming, that is beyond anything the conspiracies could ever offer. Because in the end, the truest truth, the deepest reality - it's not some abstract idea or hidden agenda, but the raw, pulsing fact of our interconnectedness, our inextricable enmeshment in the web of life itself.

That's the great irony of the journey out of the rabbit hole, the cosmic joke at the heart of it all. That in setting out to uncover some grand, nefarious conspiracy - we end up discovering a conspiracy of an entirely different sort. A conspiracy of dandelions pushing through cracks in the sidewalk, of strangers' smiles on the bus, of shared meals and shared struggles and shared dreams. The constant, quiet conspiracy of the universe to wake us up to the miracle of our own belonging, to the shimmering web of wonder and woe that entangles us all.

And it's in that entanglement, that enmeshment, that we find the truest sense of purpose, the deepest fount of meaning and mission. Not in the pursuit of some abstract, disembodied truth - but in the sacred, everyday work of tending to the relationships that sustain us, of mending the ruptures in the fabric of community, of fighting for a world where all of us can thrive and flourish and belong.

So if there's one thing I've learned in this long, strange trip out of the echo chamber and into embodied, engaged living - it's that the real revolution, the only one that truly matters, starts right here, right now, in the radical reclamation of our own rootedness, our own kinship with the world around us. It starts with the daily alchemy of presence and care, with the slow, steady weaving of a reality that is more generous, more life-affirming than any conspiracy theory could ever dream of.

And it's a revolution that is always, already underway - in the cracks and crevices of this beautiful, broken world, in the countless tiny acts of awakening and resistance that are forever rippling out from hearts and hearths and headwaters. We need only tap into that current, that quiet groundswell of regeneration - and let it carry us home to our own wildness, our own belonging, our own power to conjure new realities from the compost of the old.

So let's get on with it, shall we? Let's hit the road with our hearts on our sleeves and our hands in the dirt, ready to stumble and fumble our way towards a world of raucous resilience, of stubborn beauty, of impossible, indomitable life. There's a new dawn waiting, just beyond the next bend - and I don't know about you, but I don't want to miss a single fractal minute of it.

The rabbit hole is in the rearview now, receding into the distance like some half-remembered dream. And ahead, the horizon stretches out in every direction, shimmering with possibility, with the promise of a million different futures waiting to be born. Let's go meet them, shall we? With open eyes and open hearts, with the wild, defiant joy of travellers who know that the real adventure - the only adventure - is always, already here.

8 GUIDING OTHERS OUT

As I've been moving along on this journey out of the rabbit hole, as I've been navigating my way through the twists and turns of this new existential landscape - I've started to notice something, this growing awareness, this budding realization, that my story - this wild, meandering tale of descent and redemption, of losing myself and finding myself anew - it's not just my story.

No, the more I look around, the more I really see, the more I realize that there are so many others out there who are still trapped in that digital labyrinth, still wandering through the looking-glass world of conspiracy and delusion. From the people I love the most, the friends and family who have been by my side through thick and thin, to the strangers I encounter in the wild, untamed backwaters of the internet - I see so many fellow travelers who are grappling with the same forces that once haunted my own mind, the same specters of suspicion and isolation and existential vertigo.

And seeing this, really taking it in with the full force of my being - it's like a lightning bolt, like a clarion call from the depths of my soul. Because I realize, with a certainty that goes beyond any conspiracy or ideology, that this journey I've been on - this long, strange trip out of the rabbit hole and into the light of embodied, engaged living - it's not just for me. No, the insights I've gleaned, the hard-won wisdom I've earned - it's not meant to be hoarded like some kind of secret treasure, hidden away from the world behind a veil of silence and self-preservation.

This story, this experience - it's a gift, a sacred offering that I've been entrusted with for a reason. And that reason, I'm starting to understand with every fiber of my being, is to share it, to hold it out like a beacon of hope and possibility to all those who are still lost in the wilderness, still searching for a way out of the echo chamber and into a more authentic, more fully human way of being in the world.

Because the thing is, when you've been to the bottom of the rabbit hole and back again, when you've seen the darkness and the despair that lurks in those depths - you can't unsee it. You can't just walk away and pretend like it never happened, like there aren't countless others still trapped in that abyss, gasping for air and grasping for a lifeline. No, once you've been there, once you've tasted the bitter fruits of conspiracy and delusion - you have a responsibility, a sacred duty, to reach back and offer a helping hand to those who are still lost in the labyrinth.

And so, as I've continued on this path of recovery and reintegration, as I've continued to peel back the layers of my own psyche and rebuild a life on the solid ground of reality - I've started to turn my attention outward, to focus not just on my own healing but on the healing of the collective, the mending of the torn fabric of our shared social world.

I've started to reflect deeply, to really sit with the questions of what I've learned on this journey, what insights and practices have been most crucial in my own process of disengagement and recovery. I've started to excavate the key turning points, the watershed moments where the spell of the echo chamber started to crack and the light of reason began to seep through. I've started to catalogue the strategies and tools that proved most effective in rebuilding my sense of reality, in reclaiming my mental health and my capacity for critical thought.

And as I've done this work of self-reflection and self-inquiry, as I've started to distill the essence of my experience into something that can be shared, something that can be offered up as a guide or a roadmap for others - I've come to understand that the journey out of the rabbit hole is not a one-size-fits-all proposition. No, just as each of us spirals into the vortex of conspiracy in our own unique way, shaped by our own particular mix of circumstances and psychology - so too must each of us find our own path back out, our own way of untangling the knots of delusion and reclaiming our birthright as creatures of truth and reason.

There is no universal formula, no ten-step program or silver bullet that can instantly shatter the hold of the echo chamber. The journey of awakening, of liberation from the prison of our own minds - it's a messy, non-linear, profoundly personal process, one that unfolds in its own time and its own way for each individual who undertakes it.

But even so, even in the midst of all that complexity and idiosyncrasy - there are certain threads, certain motifs that seem to weave through all the stories of those who have found their way out of the rabbit hole and back into the light. There are certain core principles and practices that, while they may manifest differently for each of us, seem to be key to the process of disengagement and recovery.

And chief among these, the one that stands out like a beacon in the fog, is the cultivation of mindfulness - the simple but profoundly transformative practice of learning to observe our own thoughts and reactions with a sense of curiosity, with a willingness to sit in the discomfort of not-knowing and not-controlling. Because the thing about conspiratorial thinking, about the kind of all-consuming suspicion that characterizes life in the rabbit hole - is that it thrives on certainty, on the false comfort of a world neatly divided into good and evil, us and them.

To break free from that, to start to loosen the grip of those patterns of thought - we have to be willing to sit with the anxiety of ambiguity, to learn to tolerate the cognitive dissonance that comes from holding multiple perspectives at once. We have to develop the capacity to watch our own minds, to notice when we're getting hooked by a particularly tantalizing theory or a especially dire prediction - and then, in that noticing, to create just a little bit of space, a little bit of distance between ourselves and the thought.

It's in that space, that tiny gap between impulse and reaction - that choice lies. The choice to buy into the conspiracy or to question it, to get swept up in the fever dream or to plant our feet on the solid ground of what is real, what is verifiable, what is true beyond the shadow of a doubt. And the more we practice creating that space, the more we develop that muscle of mindful awareness - the easier it becomes to make that choice, to steer our minds away from the siren song of delusion and back towards the safe harbor of reason and reality.
But mindfulness, as powerful as it is, is not the whole story. No, to truly navigate our way out of the echo chamber - we need a whole toolkit, a whole repertoire of skills and strategies for engaging with the world of information in a more discerning, more critical way. We need to

become agents of our own media literacy, learning to question the sources and claims we encounter with a keen and incisive eye.

This means developing the habit of intellectual humility, of being willing to say "I don't know" in the face of complex or ambiguous information. It means learning to seek out multiple perspectives, to triangulate the truth by consulting a range of credible sources. It means cultivating a healthy skepticism, a willingness to sit with uncertainty rather than latching onto the first explanation that comes along and satisfies our need for a tidy narrative.

And perhaps most importantly, it means learning to ground our sense of reality not just in the abstract realm of ideas and information, but in the concrete, flesh-and-blood world of lived experience and embodied relationship. Because the echo chamber, for all its intensity and allure, is ultimately a place of profound disconnection - from our own bodies, from the natural world, from the web of community that sustains and nourishes us.

To truly break its spell, to truly find our way back to wholeness and health - we need to plug ourselves back into that web, to re-root ourselves in the soil of the real. We need to make a conscious effort to spend time offline, to engage in activities that bring us into contact with the physical world and the other beings who inhabit it. We need to prioritize face-to-face connection, building relationships of depth and authenticity that can serve as a lifeline when the digital waters get choppy.

And we need to be willing to speak our truth, to share our stories of struggle and redemption with others. Because there is an immense power in breaking the silence, in naming the experiences that so often get shrouded in shame and secrecy. By speaking out, by offering our own hard-won insights and extending a compassionate hand to others - we help to weave a new narrative, a new possibility for what life can be like outside the rabbit hole.

Of course, it's important to approach these conversations with care and discernment, to meet people where they are and to respect the deeply personal nature of the journey out of the rabbit hole. Challenging someone's beliefs head-on, trying to argue them out of their convictions - it rarely works, and often only leads to further entrenchment.

By focusing on connection rather than conversion, by prioritizing the building of trust and the sharing of vulnerability - we can create the conditions for genuine dialogue, for the kind of soul-to-soul exchange that has the power to melt even the most rigid of ideological stances. By asking open, honest questions and listening with the ears of the heart, we can plant seeds of doubt and curiosity that may take root and blossom in their own time.

And above all, by embodying the kind of grounded presence and compassionate wisdom that comes from having walked this path ourselves - we can serve as living proof that there is another way, that it is possible to find meaning and belonging outside the confines of the echo chamber. We can be the lighthouse keepers, the way showers, the trail guides for all those who are ready to take that first tentative step into the unknown.

Ultimately, the journey out of the rabbit hole is a hero's journey that each of us must undertake in our own way and in our own time. No one can walk the path for us, and no one can short-circuit the often painful but always necessary process of confronting our own shadows and reclaiming our own agency and authority.

But what we can do, what we must do if we are to heal the great wound of disconnection and distrust that is tearing at the fabric of our world - is to light the way for each other, to share our stories and our tools and our hard-earned wisdom like precious gems strewn along the path. We can be the community of recovery, the fellowship of the disenchanted, the great welcoming committee for all those who are ready to cross the threshold and come home to themselves.

And in doing this work, in taking up this mantle of mentorship and guidance - we not only help to heal others, but we continue to heal ourselves. Because the journey out of the rabbit hole is not a destination but an ongoing practice, a daily choice to keep showing up to reality in all its complexity and heartbreak and beauty. By committing ourselves to this path, by vowing to walk it with others - we ensure our own continued growth and liberation, even as we contribute to the mending of the world.

So to all those who may be reading these words from within the labyrinth of conspiratorial thinking, to all those who feel the first stirrings of doubt and the first longing for a different way of being - know that you are not alone, and you are not crazy for wanting to find your way out. The path is waiting for you, and there are fellow travelers ready to walk it with you, step by stumbling step.

It won't be easy, and it won't be quick. The journey out of the echo chamber is a long and winding road, full of switchbacks and pitfalls and moments of existential uncertainty. But it is a journey worth taking, a hero's quest in the truest sense of the word. Because in liberating yourself from the prison of your own mind, you not only reclaim your own connection - but you help to reclaim the connection of us all.

So take heart, weary traveler. The new dawn is waiting, just beyond the next bend in the road. And we - the community of those who have walked this path before you - we are here, holding the lantern of hope and possibility, ready to light your way.

Step by step, story by story, heart to heart - we will find our way out of the darkness and into the light of a new day, a new world, a new way of being that is grounded in truth, in love, in the unshakeable knowing of our own interconnectedness.

The journey begins anew with every choice, every breath, every courageous act of reaching out and saying "I'm ready to come back". So let us begin, you and I.

Let's hit the road. Let's leave the rabbit hole behind and strike out for the territories of the real, the true, the unimaginably alive. There's a world out there waiting to be rediscovered, and it's more vivid and enchanting than any conspiracy ever dreamed.

I'll see you on the other side, my friend. May the wind be always at your back. The adventure of a lifetime awaits.